PETERSON
FIELD GUIDE
SERIES®

BIRDING BY EAR

EASTERN
AND CENTRAL
NORTH AMERICA

A Guide to Bird-song Identification

Richard K. Walton
and
Robert W. Lawson

with an editor's note by
ROGER TORY PETERSON

Illustrations by
JOHN SILL

Houghton
Mifflin
Company

BOSTON
NEW YORK

Editor's note copyright © 1989 by Roger Tory Peterson.
Text copyright © 1990 by Richard K. Walton and Robert W. Lawson.
Narration copyright ℗ 1990 by Richard K. Walton and
Robert W. Lawson.
Recordings copyright ℗ 1990 by the Library of Natural Sounds,
Cornell Laboratory of Ornithology, Ithaca, NY, and the Borror
Laboratory of Bioacoustics, Ohio State University.
Illustrations copyright © 1990 by Houghton Mifflin Company.

All rights reserved.

For information about permission to reproduce selections from
this book, write to Permissions, Houghton Mifflin Company,
215 Park Avenue South, New York, New York 10003

PETERSON FIELD GUIDES and
PETERSON FIELD GUIDE SERIES
are registered trademarks of Houghton Mifflin Company.

Printed in the United States of America

G 13 12 11 10 9 8 7 6 5

CREDITS

Birding by Ear was created by Richard Walton and Robert Lawson.

Bird-song samples were supplied by the Laboratory of Ornithology at Cornell University and the Borror Laboratory of Bioacoustics at Ohio State University.

Background bird songs used in the introduction are from the recording *Dawn Chorus — Birds of Morning Pro Musica* (available on cassette from WGBH, 125 Western Ave., Boston, MA 02134). The Blue Jay's imitation of the Red-shouldered Hawk was provided by the Florida Museum of Natural History, Gainesville, Florida.

Produced at Blue Jay Recording Studio in Carlisle, Massachusetts.
Engineers: Mark Tanzer and Mark Wessel

Drawings by John Sill

Cover Photograph copyright © by Ron Austing

ABOUT THE AUTHORS

RICHARD K. WALTON is a teacher, writer, and naturalist. His publications include *Bird Finding in New England* and *Birds of the Sudbury River Valley*.
ROBERT W. LAWSON is a bird enthusiast and is the owner of Blue Jay Recording Studio.

EDITOR'S NOTE

Birding by Ear is a unique and important new tool for birders. Now they can easily master one of the most useful and difficult field skills — the ability to recognize birds by their songs and calls. Just as my Field Guide shows what to *look* for, *Birding by Ear* points out exactly what to *listen* for to tell one bird from another. As the Field Guide groups birds by visual similarity, *Birding by Ear* groups them by acoustic similarity. Dick Walton and Bob Lawson have arranged eighty-five common species into seventeen intelligible learning groups, such as "whistlers," "chippers and trillers," "name-sayers," and "mimics." The entertaining and educational narrative does the same job as the arrows in my Field Guide, pinpointing the precise differences between similar species. The songs themselves are recorded to the highest acoustic standards and are a delight to listen to.

Birding by Ear can enable anyone to become a better birder. Use it in conjunction with the Peterson *Field Guide to Bird Songs*, which provides a thorough catalog of the songs and calls of the familiar birds of eastern and central North America (a *Field Guide to Western Bird Songs* is also available). *Birding by Ear* may well become as essential to you as your Field Guide and binoculars.

Roger Tory Peterson

To the memory of Will
  RKW

For Barrett, my best birding companion
  RWL

ACKNOWLEDGMENTS

The authors would like to express their appreciation to James Baird, Richard Forster, and Wayne Petersen, who reviewed and commented on the manuscript. Our special thanks to Andrea Priori, Bill Evans, and John Bower at Cornell's Laboratory of Ornithology and Sandra Gaunt, Dr. Andrew Thompson, and Gregg Zuberbier at Ohio State's Borror Laboratory of Bioacoustics, all of whom provided us with excellent song samples. Thanks also go to Mark Tanzer and Mark Wessel for their long hours of recording and mixing this production at Blue Jay Studio, and to Mark Mekker of Eastern Standard Productions for cassette duplication. Our appreciation also goes to Dr. William Hardy of the Florida Museum of Natural History and to WGBH's Susy Cheston and to *Morning Pro Musica*'s Robert J. Lurtsema.

We also want to thank Roger Tory Peterson for his interest in the project, and John Sill for his bird sketches.

Harry Foster, our editor at Houghton Mifflin, deserves special mention; it was his enthusiasm for our idea that brought this guide to fruition.

Last, but not least, we would like to thank Adelaide Walton and Janet Lawson for their support, encouragement, and suggestions.

INTRODUCTION

Birding is a deceptively simple pastime. Equipped with binoculars and field guide, aficionados can seemingly go anywhere on Earth and enjoy the pleasures of a few hours in the field. Yet to the uninitiated, experienced birders regularly perform feats that are little short of miraculous. A hawk barely discernible in the distance, a warbler flitting in the treetops, even a mere squeak in the reeds are identified with confidence. In actuality, there is nothing magical about the experts' keen perception; their skills have been developed through hours of study and many seasons of field work.

Half the battle of effective field identification is learning what birds to expect, including the commonplace, the unusual, and the rarities. The other component in the experts' bag of tricks is the ability to use cues, both visual and auditory, from the birds themselves. Most beginners concentrate all of their efforts on the visual cues—after all, they reason, this is bird *watching!*—and field guides provide an efficient system for learning the various plumages and field marks. Mastering the auditory clues has been more difficult, because there has not been a comparable learning system available. Although field guides often include detailed notes on vocalizations, reading about a bird's song, or viewing it on a sonagram, can not convey the essence of the song. Most bird-song recordings are simply collections of the songs and calls of different species. These collections constitute a valuable reference, but they do not provide techniques for distinguishing and remembering songs.

Birding by Ear addresses these issues by focusing on two basic tasks. First, we have tried to create an audio format that will help you to develop a "basic vocabulary" of bird song for birds found in eastern and central North America. To this end, we have selected widespread and vocal birds and grouped them largely on the basis of similarity of song. Just as seeing side-by-side illustrations of the similar-looking Purple Finch and House Finch allows you to contrast the identifying visual field marks, hearing the finches' songs in close succession enables you to focus on diagnostic differences between the two vocalizations. We call this technique "pairing." Besides pairing, we have used phonetics, comparative ideas, and mnemonics to create groups that provide a context for learning the various songs and calls. We believe that anyone who spends a reasonable amount of time with the tapes will obtain a working knowledge of the songs and calls of eighty-five common species. This will familiarize birders with many, if not most, of the songs and calls they will hear in the field. There will, however, be species in your area that are not covered in this guide. And this leads to our second goal. *Birding by Ear* provides a system for learning bird song in general, including unfamiliar and new songs and calls. As you proceed through the learning groups you will develop techniques and vocabulary useful in characterizing and recalling bird song. With some practice, you should be able to apply these concepts to learn to recognize the songs and calls of many other species.

Just as there is nothing magical about the visual skills of the expert birder in the field, there is little mystery to learning bird song. Work with the tapes and apply your learning in the field. Also, be prepared for variations in bird song. Just as the bird in the field may not *look* exactly like the one in your field guide, the song may *sound* somewhat different from the samples on the tapes.

It is our hope that learning bird song will enhance not only your field skills but also your appreciation of the world of birds.

Dick Walton and Bob Lawson
Concord, Massachusetts

LEARNING GROUPS

Cassette 1, Side A

INTRODUCTION

MIMICS
  Northern Mockingbird
  Brown Thrasher
  Gray Catbird
WOODPECKERS
  Downy Woodpecker
  Hairy Woodpecker
  Red-headed
    Woodpecker
  Red-bellied Woodpecker
  Northern Flicker
  Pileated Woodpecker
  Belted Kingfisher

Cassette 1, Side B

SING-SONGERS
  American Robin
  Scarlet Tanager
  Summer Tanager
  Rose-breasted Grosbeak
  Red-eyed Vireo
  Yellow-throated Vireo
HAWKS
  Broad-winged Hawk
  Red-tailed Hawk
  Red-shouldered Hawk
CHIPPERS AND TRILLERS
  Swamp Sparrow
  Chipping Sparrow
  Dark-eyed Junco
  Pine Warbler
HIGH-PITCHERS
  Cedar Waxwing
  Brown-headed Cowbird
  Eastern Kingbird
  European Starling

Cassette 2, Side A

WHISTLERS
  Northern Cardinal
  Tufted Titmouse
  Northern Oriole
  Eastern Meadowlark
  Field Sparrow
  White-throated Sparrow
OWLS AND A DOVE
  Great Horned Owl
  Barred Owl
  Eastern Screech-Owl
  Mourning Dove
SIMPLE VOCALIZATIONS
  Great Crested
    Flycatcher
  Acadian Flycatcher
  White-breasted
    Nuthatch
  American Woodcock
  Green-backed Heron
  Black-crowned
    Night-Heron
  Ring-necked Pheasant
COMPLEX
VOCALIZATIONS
  Bobolink
  House Wren
  American Goldfinch

Cassette 2, Side B

NAME-SAYERS
  Whip-poor-will
  Chuck-will's-widow
  Black-capped Chickadee
  Carolina Chickadee
  Eastern Phoebe
  Eastern Wood-Pewee
  Killdeer
  Northern Bobwhite

WARBLING SONGSTERS
- House Finch
- Purple Finch
- Warbling Vireo
- Orchard Oriole

COMMONERS
- Canada Goose
- American Crow
- Blue Jay
- House Sparrow
- Red-winged Blackbird
- Common Grackle
- Song Sparrow

Cassette 3, Side A

WOOD WARBLERS AND A WREN
- Black-and-white Warbler
- Ovenbird
- Kentucky Warbler
- Carolina Wren
- Hooded Warbler
- Common Yellowthroat
- Yellow Warbler
- Northern Parula
- Black-throated Green Warbler
- American Redstart

THRUSHES
- Wood Thrush
- Veery
- Hermit Thrush

UNUSUAL VOCALIZATIONS
- Ruffed Grouse
- American Woodcock
- American Bittern

MISCELLANEOUS VOCALIZATIONS
- Chimney Swift
- White-eyed Vireo
- Eastern Bluebird
- Rufous-sided Towhee

Cassette 3, Side B

HABITAT GROUPINGS

EASTERN FORESTS

Forest Edges
- Blue Jay
- Wood Thrush
- Gray Catbird
- Downy Woodpecker
- Eastern Wood-Pewee
- Rose-breasted Grosbeak
- Eastern Phoebe
- Great Crested Flycatcher
- Red-eyed Vireo
- American Goldfinch

Forest Interiors
- Ruffed Grouse
- White-breasted Nuthatch
- Broad-winged Hawk
- Ovenbird
- Barred Owl
- Hairy Woodpecker
- Veery
- Black-throated Green Warbler
- Black-and-white Warbler
- House Wren
- Scarlet Tanager

Throughout
- American Crow
- Northern Oriole
- Red-tailed Hawk
- American Robin
- Eastern Screech-Owl
- Common Grackle

FRESHWATER WETLANDS
- Swamp Sparrow
- American Bittern
- Red-winged Blackbird
- Green-backed Heron
- Belted Kingfisher
- Black-crowned Night-Heron
- Canada Goose

SOUTHERN FORESTS
- Red-bellied Woodpecker
- Summer Tanager
- Tufted Titmouse
- Carolina Chickadee
- Orchard Oriole
- Kentucky Warbler
- Hooded Warbler
- Yellow-throated Vireo
- Pileated Woodpecker
- Acadian Flycatcher

NORTHERN FORESTS
- Cedar Waxwing
- White-throated Sparrow
- Black-capped Chickadee
- Purple Finch
- American Redstart
- Hermit Thrush
- Warbling Vireo
- Dark-eyed Junco

HEDGEROWS AND THICKETS
- Northern Bobwhite
- Song Sparrow
- Common Yellowthroat
- Brown Thrasher
- Northern Mockingbird
- Yellow Warbler
- White-eyed Vireo
- Northern Cardinal
- Carolina Wren

OLD FIELDS AND OPEN FIELDS
- Eastern Kingbird
- Eastern Meadowlark
- Field Sparrow
- Ring-necked Pheasant
- Bobolink
- Killdeer
- American Woodcock

OAK-PINE WOODLANDS
- Red-headed Woodpecker
- Red-shouldered Hawk
- Chipping Sparrow
- Pine Warbler
- Mourning Dove
- Chuck-will's-widow
- Northern Parula
- Eastern Bluebird
- Northern Flicker
- Great Horned Owl
- Whip-poor-will
- Rufous-sided Towhee

URBAN PARKS
- Chimney Swift
- Brown-headed Cowbird
- House Finch
- House Sparrow
- European Starling

CASSETTE 1, SIDE A

Mimics

All three species in this group are members of the mimic thrush family. Their songs are fairly complex and include a wide range of phrases, some melodious, others harsh. The key to species identification is the number of repetitions of each vocal phrase.

NORTHERN MOCKINGBIRD

Mimus polyglottos

(p. 218)*

Habitat: Edges of rural and suburban clearings with associated brushy tangles, preferably with a ready supply of berries and fruits. This bird sings from open, high perches throughout the year and even on bright, moonlit nights during the nesting season.

Voice: Numerous combinations of melodious and harsh phrases, each normally repeated three or more times. *Call note*: A loud, harsh *tchak*. This bird mimics with precision a wide variety of bird songs, as well as other natural and man-made sounds.

Notes:

---

*Page numbers refer to species descriptions in *A Field Guide to the Birds of Eastern and Central North America*, by Roger Tory Peterson (Houghton Mifflin, 1980).

BROWN THRASHER

Toxostoma rufum

(p. 218)

Habitat: Woodland edges, dry hillsides and thickets, and hedgerows in rural areas, at times near human habitations. Although it is normally shy and secretive, this species often sings from an exposed perch.

Voice: A series of rich, whistle-like phrases given two or three times (one or two repetitions); normally less varied than the Mocker's. *Call note:* A low, harsh *smack* and a three-noted whistle.

Notes:

GRAY CATBIRD

Dumetella carolinensis

(p. 218)

Habitat: Dense thickets and undergrowth. This bird often sings from its preferred habitat and thus stays out of sight.

Voice: Song a disjointed medley of harsh, squeaky, and nasal phrases with occasional sweet notes. Each phrase is normally given only once.
Call note: A harsh, catlike *meeoow*; also a harsh, crackling series of notes.

Notes:

Woodpeckers

This group includes the six common woodpeckers of eastern North America. While the drumming is not always diagnostic, each of these species has other characteristic vocalizations.

DOWNY WOODPECKER

Picoides pubescens

(p. 192)

Habitat: Fairly common in smaller woodlots, including those in parks and urban and suburban neighborhoods.
Voice: A descending whinny. *Call note:* A flat *pik*.
Notes:

HAIRY WOODPECKER

Picoides villosus

(p. 192)

Habitat: Resident of large wooded tracts; less often found around human habitations.
Voice: A low, even-pitched rattle. *Call note:* A loud, sharp *peek*.
Notes:

RED-HEADED WOODPECKER

Melanerpes erythrocephalus

(p. 188)

Habitat: Open areas at the edges of woodlands in both rural and suburban locales.
Voice: A relatively high, raspy *queer, queer* . . . Note the beginning "qu" sound.
Notes:

RED-BELLIED WOODPECKER

Melanerpes carolinus

(p. 190)

Habitat: A wide variety of woodlands, including riverine bottomlands, parks, and suburbs.
Voice: A relatively low, repetitious *churr, churr, churr* . . . Note the trilled quality of this nasal vocalization.
Notes:

NORTHERN FLICKER

Colaptes auratus

(p. 190)

Habitat: A wide variety of wooded areas; essentially wherever suitable nesting cavities exist.
Voice: A loud, repetitious *wick, wick, wick,* typically held at one pitch through much of the call; also a softer *week-a, week-a, week-a. Call note: Kleeyer,* or *eeyer.*
Notes:

PILEATED WOODPECKER

Dryocopus pileatus

(p. 188)

Habitat: A variety of woodlands, including some suburban areas.
Voice: A loud *kik, kik, kik;* similar to that of the Northern Flicker but louder and often rising and falling in pitch and tempo throughout the call.
Notes:

BELTED KINGFISHER

Ceryle alcyon

(p. 186)

Habitat: Normally found near wetlands, including freshwater ponds, streams, lakes, and coastal tidal areas.
Voice: *Flight call:* A nonmusical rattle.
Notes:

CASSETTE 1, SIDE B

Sing-songers

These birds are grouped together because of the up-and-down (rising and falling) inflections and rhythmic patterns of their songs.

AMERICAN ROBIN

Turdus migratorius

(p. 220)

Habitat: Suburban neighborhoods and parks, open forests, and woodland edges.
Voice: Song a lengthy carol resembling *cheerily, cheer-up, cheerily . . .* ; three or more phrases often grouped together. *Call notes:* Various, including a whinny, chuck notes, a rapid *tut, tut, tut,* and a lisping flight note. Often sings at daybreak and dusk.
Notes:

SCARLET TANAGER

Piranga olivacea

(p. 260)

Habitat: Woodlands, including deciduous and mixed forests, parks, and well-planted neighborhoods.
Voice: Song similar to that of the American Robin but with a burry quality. *Call note:* A diagnostic *chick-burr;* sometimes just *chick.*
Notes:

SUMMER TANAGER

Piranga rubra

(p. 260)

Habitat: Upland and streamside pine-oak woodlands.
Voice: Song is like the Scarlet Tanager's but less burry. *Call note:* A rapid *piki-tucki-tuck* or *pik-a-tuck.*
Notes:

ROSE-BREASTED GROSBEAK

Pheucticus ludovicianus

(p. 276)

Habitat: Associations of rich woodlands and shrubby, more open areas, in both rural and suburban situations.
Voice: Exuberant whistled phrases, run together to create a lengthy, rich, robin-like song. *Call note:* A distinctive metallic *chink* (often interspersed with the song).
Notes:

RED-EYED VIREO

Vireo olivaceus

(p. 226)

Habitat: Most deciduous or mixed woodlands in rural and suburban situations. Song often given from high in the canopy.
Voice: Song has a monotonous, rising and falling rhythm; phrases often evenly spaced with regular pauses: *here I am, where are you? here I am, where are you?* Highly repetitious, often continuing for a long time. *Call note:* A whiny *chwey.*
Notes:

YELLOW-THROATED VIREO

Vireo flavifrons

(p. 228)

Habitat: Mature, deciduous woodlands, often in association with water.
Voice: Song similar to Red-eyed Vireo's but slower and lower, with lengthy pauses between phrases; has a burry quality: *three-a, three-a . . .*
Notes:

Hawks

This group includes the three common buteos of eastern North America.

BROAD-WINGED HAWK

Buteo platypterus

(p. 156)

Habitat: Deciduous and mixed forest.
Voice: A high-pitched, thin whistle: *peeee-eeeee*.
Notes:

RED-TAILED HAWK

Buteo jamaicensis

(p. 154)

Habitat: A variety of habitats, including woodland edges and fields with scattered groves of trees.
Voice: A husky, descending scream—*keeeeeeer*; usually one long, down-slurred syllable.
Notes:

RED-SHOULDERED HAWK

Buteo lineatus

(p. 156)

Habitat: Moist, deciduous woodlands, often associated with swamps or river bottoms.
Voice: A two-syllable, repetitious *kee-yer, kee-yer, kee-yer* . . . Each phrase is generally shorter and less husky than the Red-tail's call.
Notes:

Chippers and Trillers

All four species in this group give trills. Habitat associations and visual clues should be combined with song characteristics to confirm the identity of these species.

SWAMP SPARROW

Melospiza georgiana

(p. 280)

Habitat: Freshwater wetlands, especially cattail marshes, sedgy swamps, and river meadows.
Voice: A relatively slow trill, sometimes slow enough to count individual chips; at times, a faster, reedy trill.
Notes:

CHIPPING SPARROW

Spizella passerina

(p. 280)

Habitat: Woodland edges and forest clearings; commonly found around suburban residences, golf courses, and rural farmlands.
Voice: A rapid, dry trill.
Notes:

DARK-EYED JUNCO

Junco hyemalis

(p. 266)

Habitat: Nests in northern coniferous and mixed forests; winters in weed fields and thickets.
Voice: A sweeter and more musical trill than the Chipping Sparrow's, sometimes with a bell-like quality; at other times burry. *Call notes:* A series of flat, clicking notes.
Notes:

PINE WARBLER

Dendroica pinus

(p. 238)

Habitat: Pine woodlands and barrens.
Voice: A loose, musical trill, often with a lazy, soft quality.
Notes:

High-pitchers

The birds in this group all have relatively high-pitched notes in their vocalizations.

CEDAR WAXWING

Bombycilla cedrorum

(p. 224)

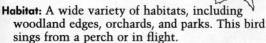

Habitat: A wide variety of habitats, including woodland edges, orchards, and parks. This bird sings from a perch or in flight.
Voice: A high-pitched, buzzy *zeee, zeee* ...
Notes:

BROWN-HEADED COWBIRD

Molothrus ater

(p. 252)

Habitat: During the breeding season this species, which lays its eggs in other birds' nests, is found in various habitats, including wetlands, uplands, and neighborhood settings. Once confined to the prairies, this cowbird has spread throughout the lower 48 states.
Voice: A high-pitched *bubble, bubble, zee. Call notes:* A high-pitched note, often given in flight; also a sputtering chatter.
Notes:

EASTERN KINGBIRD

Tyrannus tyrannus

(p. 194)

Habitat: Most open areas with prominent perches, including edges of wetlands and rural farmlands. Vocalizations are given in flight and from a perch.
Voice: A series of stuttered and punctuated notes sounding like electrical sparks jumping between two wires: *dtzee, dtzee, dtzeet*.
Notes:

EUROPEAN STARLING

Sturnus vulgaris

(p. 256)

Habitat: Most habitats, including cities. Sings from a perch.
Voice: A series of high-pitched, squeaky squeals and various lower clucks and clicks; also a wolf whistle. Able to mimic a variety of birds.
Notes:

CASSETTE 2, SIDE A

Whistlers

This group comprises birds with clear, whistle-like songs.

NORTHERN CARDINAL

Cardinalis cardinalis

(p. 268)

Habitat: Thickets and brushy areas. Sings throughout the year.
Voice: Various whistled phrases, often including either a down-slurred *cheer* or an up-slurred *wheet*, followed by a series of repetitious notes; also *purty, purty, purty* . . . and/or *quoit, quoit, quoit* . . . *Call note:* A distinctive, loud chip.
Notes:

TUFTED TITMOUSE

Parus bicolor

(p. 210)

Habitat: Woodlands.
Voice: A whistled song with two basic variations: a slightly down-slurred *here, here, here . . .* and a two-noted *chiva, chiva, chiva . . . Call notes:* Various high-pitched, nasal whistles and wheezes.
Notes:

NORTHERN ORIOLE

Icterus galbula

(p. 258)

Habitat: Wooded areas, especially shade trees of parks and residential neighborhoods.
Voice: Various flutelike, rich whistles; there is considerable rhythmic and melodic variation among individuals. *Call note:* A harsh chatter or rattle.
Notes:

EASTERN MEADOWLARK

Sturnella magna

(p. 256)

Habitat: Open, grassy fields and meadows. Often sings from a fence post or other perch in nesting territory.

Voice: Song consists of two down-slurred whistles per phrase: *spring-of-the-year* . . . ; also a distinctive guttural rattle at the end of the song.

Notes:

FIELD SPARROW

Spizella pusilla

(p. 280)

Habitat: Abandoned pastures and meadows with second-growth cover.

Voice: An accelerating whistle that ends in a trill; rhythmic pattern similar to that of a ping-pong ball dropping on a table.

Notes:

WHITE-THROATED SPARROW

Zonotrichia albicollis

(p. 278)

Habitat: Forest openings, slash areas, and thickets.
Voice: One or more introductory notes followed by a series of triplets; variable—at times *Old Sam Peabody, Peabody, Peabody* or *Sam Peabody, Peabody, Peabody. Call note:* A high, thin *tseet*.
Notes:

Owls and a Dove

Two of the owl species covered here give classic "hoots"; a third species, the screech-owl, gives a whistled whinny. Like most owls, these three species are largely nocturnal and thus are most likely to be heard between dusk and dawn. The Mourning Dove, which is not related to the owls, is included in this group because many beginners mistake its sad cooing, given during daylight hours, for an owl vocalization.

GREAT HORNED OWL

Bubo virginianus

(p. 172)

Habitat: A variety of woodland habitats, from heavily forested areas to urban parks.
Voice: Commonly five or six deep hoots, repeated several times, often with a rhythm similar to the phrase *who's awake? me, too*. At times hoots in concert with a mate or other Great Horned Owls. *Call notes:* A variety of seldom-heard screams.
Notes:

BARRED OWL

Strix varia

(p. 174)

Habitat: Woodland swamps and forests.
Voice: Eight or nine hoots: *who cooks for you, who cooks for you (all)?* Variations include *madam, who cooks for you? Call notes:* An extraordinary caterwauling may ensue when two or more Barred Owls engage in a "shouting match."
Notes:

EASTERN SCREECH-OWL

Otus asio

(p. 172)

Habitat: A variety of habitats, including orchards, river floodplains, and woodland clearings. Screech-owls occur fairly regularly in residential settings.
Voice: A mournful, descending whinny; also a whistled tremolo on one pitch.
Notes:

MOURNING DOVE

Zenaida macroura

(p. 180)

Habitat: Most habitats except deep forests. Sings just before dawn and throughout the day.
Voice: A mournful, five-syllable phrase: *oo-ah, whoo, whoo, whoo,* the last three coos on the same pitch. Wings often produce a whir sounding like a fluttered whistle when the bird takes off.
Notes:

Simple Vocalizations

These seven species are grouped together because they all have fairly simple, single- or two-noted songs or calls that are frequently repeated.

GREAT CRESTED FLYCATCHER

Myiarchus crinitus

(p. 194)

Habitat: Deciduous and mixed woodlands in both suburban and rural areas. Often calls from the cover of woodlands.
Voice: Most commonly heard vocalization is a repetitious, ascending *wheep, wheep, wheep;* also a lower-pitched, trilled *prrrreet*.
Notes:

ACADIAN FLYCATCHER

Empidonax virescens

(p. 198)

Habitat: Mature deciduous forests.
Voice: A sharp, abrupt two-noted *peet-seet* or *peet-suh*, with the second note higher; repetitious, with little variation. *Call notes:* A series of *pip* notes.
Notes:

WHITE-BREASTED NUTHATCH

Sitta carolinensis

(p. 212)

Habitat: Woodlands, including parks, neighborhoods, and orchards.
Voice: The most commonly heard vocalization is the call: a nasal *ank, ank, ank* ... Song is also somewhat nasal—a rapidly repeated single note, *whi, whi, whi* ...
Notes:

AMERICAN WOODCOCK

Scolopax minor

(p. 124)

Habitat: Wet areas, including openings in the forest, alder thickets, and river meadows.
Voice: This bird is included here because its introductory notes are a simple, repeated, nasal *peent, peent, peent* ... Continuation of song, given in flight, includes whistles and chirps. (See "Unusual Vocalizations," p. 57.)
Notes:

GREEN-BACKED HERON

Butorides striatus

(p. 104)

Habitat: Nests in a variety of woodlands, near fresh or salt water.
Voice: The most commonly heard vocalization, often given in flight or when flushed, is a loud *skeeow*.
Notes:

BLACK-CROWNED NIGHT-HERON

Nycticorax nycticorax

(p. 104)

Habitat: Coastal woodlands bordering marshes; also inland around wooded swamps and marshes, even streams and ponds.
Voice: Flight call, often heard at dusk, is a harsh, barking *quwalk, quwalk* . . .
Notes:

RING-NECKED PHEASANT

Phasianus colchicus

(p. 144)

Habitat: Agricultural areas with good cover and old fields.
Voice: A loud, two-noted squawk, followed by a wing whir.
Notes:

Complex Vocalizations

All three species included here have complex vocalizations.

BOBOLINK

Dolichonyx oryzivorus

(p. 256)

Habitat: Fields and meadows with tall grass cover.
Voice: A bubbly flight song that gains speed and complexity as it moves along. *Call note:* A relatively soft *plink, plink,* often given in flight.
Notes:

HOUSE WREN

Troglodytes aedon

(p. 214)

Habitat: Woodland edges and slash areas, thickets, and around human habitation.
Voice: Rising and falling, exuberant bursts of bubbling song. *Call note:* A scolding chatter.
Notes:

AMERICAN GOLDFINCH

Carduelis tristis

(p. 272)

Habitat: Wooded edges of weedy fields.
Voice: Song a lively, high-pitched series of chips, twitters, and trills. *Flight call: Perchickaree, perchickaree . . . ;* also a whiny note.
Notes:

CASSETTE 2, SIDE B

Name-sayers

These birds are grouped together because their standard English name is a phonetic representation of one of their typical songs or calls.

WHIP-POOR-WILL

Caprimulgus vociferus

(p. 184)

Habitat: Deciduous woodlands, barrens, woodlots, and dry hillsides in rural areas.
Voice: A three-part *whip-poor-will*, with the second phrase comprising two syllables; the accent is on the first and last phrases. Close at hand, an additional introductory *tuck* may be heard. Repetitious; approximately one song per second. A nocturnal songster heard most commonly after dusk and during the pre-dawn hours.
Notes:

CHUCK-WILL'S-WIDOW

Caprimulgus carolinensis

(p. 184)

Habitat: Agricultural areas with scattered woodlots and low southern bottomlands. Sings from a perch, most commonly at dusk.

Voice: A four-part *chuck-will's-wid-ow*, with the accent on the third syllable; lengthier pauses between songs than in previous species. *Call note:* A low *chuck*, also given in flight.

Notes:

BLACK-CAPPED CHICKADEE

Parus atricapillus

(p. 210)

Habitat: Chiefly mixed and deciduous woodlands; fairly common in well-planted neighborhoods and parks.

Voice: Call a clear *chick-a-dee-dee-dee*, sometimes just *dee-dee-dee*; song a whistled, two-part *fee-bee* (sometimes *fee-bee-ee*); also a series of high-pitched sounds, garbled notes, and sputters.

Notes:

CAROLINA CHICKADEE

Parus carolinensis

(p. 210)

Habitat: A wide range of wooded areas, including swamps, uplands, and mountainside forests.
Voice: Call a rapid, high-pitched *chick-a-dee-dee-dee* or just *dee-dee-dee*; song a whistled, four-part *fee-bee-bee-bay*; also a series of high-pitched sounds, garbled notes, and sputters.
Notes:

EASTERN PHOEBE

Sayornis phoebe

(p. 196)

Habitat: Commonly around running water; also in suburban neighborhoods and on farms. Often sings from a favored perch.
Voice: An abrupt and emphatic *phoe-bee, phoe-bee,* at times sounding like *fee-b-lee. Call note:* A flat *chip*.
Notes:

EASTERN WOOD-PEWEE

Contopus virens

(p. 196)

Habitat: Mixed and deciduous woodlands; often sings from a perch in deep woodlands at dawn and dusk.
Voice: A plaintive whistle of three, sometimes two, syllables: *pee-a-wee* and *pee-ee* (note the rising inflection at the end of each phrase); sometimes a down-slurred *pee-yer*.
Notes:

KILLDEER

Charadrius vociferus

(p. 120)

Habitat: A wide variety of open areas, including fields and lawns. Vocalizations are given on the ground and in flight.
Voice: A repetitious *kill-deer, kill-deer* . . . ; often *ki-dee, ki-dee* . . . or *dee, dee, dee* . . .
Notes:

NORTHERN BOBWHITE

Colinus virginianus

(p. 148)

Habitat: Woodland edges and fields with brushy cover.
Voice: A strongly whistled *bob-white, bob-white . . .*; at times the second syllable is unaccompanied.
 Also, the covey call: a whistled *a-loi-he, al-loi-he . . .*
Notes:

Warbling Songsters

This group comprises birds whose songs can best be described as lengthy warbles.

HOUSE FINCH

Carpodacus mexicanus

(p. 270)

Habitat: Commonly found around human habitations in rural, suburban, and urban areas.
Voice: A lengthy, relatively high-pitched warble; more burry than the songs of others in this group. Listen for the harsh, slurred *zree* notes. *Call note:* A sweet *cheep.*
Notes:

PURPLE FINCH

Carpodacus purpureus

(p. 270)

Habitat: Coniferous or mixed woodlands, including well-planted neighborhoods, parks, and orchards.
Voice: A clear, lively warble, lacking the harsh *zree* notes of the House Finch's song; sometimes ending abruptly or with a short, downward trill. *Call note:* A flat *tick*.
Notes:

WARBLING VIREO

Vireo gilvus

(p. 226)

Habitat: Wooded banks of rivers and streams; also parks and suburban neighborhoods.
Voice: A lengthy warble, similar to the Purple Finch's song but less lively and with a more measured tempo. Listen for ending notes that rise in pitch. *Call note:* A whiny *tway, tway . . .*
Notes:

ORCHARD ORIOLE

Icterus spurius

(p. 258)

Habitat: Orchards, parks, and woodland edges.
Voice: Has been likened to that of both the Purple Finch and the American Robin; a rapid, varied series of phrases, often ending in a down-slurred *wheer* note.
Notes:

Commoners

The birds in this group are common throughout eastern North America. Several of the species included here have vocalizations that are familiar even to nonbirders.

CANADA GOOSE

Branta canadensis

(p. 44)

Habitat: Wetlands and fields.
Voice: Flock calls, given in flight and on the ground, sound like honks and barks; mated pairs give alternating honks.
Notes:

AMERICAN CROW

Corvus brachyrhynchos

(p. 206)

Habitat: Woodlands and semi-open areas.
Voice: Typical call a raucous *caw, caw, caw* . . . ; also a variety of rattles and clicks.
Notes:

BLUE JAY

Cyanocitta cristata

(p. 208)

Habitat: Woodlands, especially oak, beech, and/or pine forests.
Voice: Varied; a harsh *jay, jay, jay* . . . and a musical *queedle, queedle, queedle* . . . Also mimics local buteos.
Notes:

HOUSE SPARROW

Passer domesticus

(p. 262)

Habitat: Urban, suburban, and rural areas near human habitations.
Voice: Dry, nonmusical chirps. *Call notes:* A scolding chatter.
Notes:

RED-WINGED BLACKBIRD

Agelaius phoeniceus

(p. 252)

Habitat: Freshwater wetlands.
Voice: A distinctive *conqueree*, with the last syllable being a drawn-out trill; also a low chuck note and a high-pitched, two-noted whistle: *tse-er, tse-er*.
Notes:

COMMON GRACKLE

Quiscalus quiscula

(p. 254)

Habitat: A wide variety of habitats; nests in loose colonies, often in evergreens.
Voice: Harsh *tchack* notes; raspy, metallic squeaks; distinctly nonmusical.
Notes:

SONG SPARROW

Melospiza melodia

(p. 284)

Habitat: Fields with second-growth cover, thickets, and edges.
Voice: Three (sometimes two) introductory notes, followed by various notes and trills. Extremely variable; sometimes represented as *maids, maids, maids, put on your tea, kettle, kettle, kettle.*
Notes:

CASSETTE 3, SIDE A

Wood Warblers and a Wren

This group comprises wood warblers and a wren. The vocalizations of these birds include a variety of song types, from relatively simple two-noted phrases to complex melodies.

BLACK-AND-WHITE WARBLER

Mniotilta varia

(p. 232)

Habitat: Deciduous and mixed woodlands.
Voice: A lisping, two-noted *wee-sa, wee-sa, wee-sa* . . . ; sounds like a squeaky wheel turning round and round.
Notes:

OVENBIRD

Seiurus aurocapillus

(p. 246)

Habitat: Nests in a variety of woodlands, including dry, open deciduous forests and wet lowlands. Song often given from a low perch.
Voice: Song an emphatic *teacher, teacher, teacher* . . . ; phrases grow louder toward end of song.
Notes:

KENTUCKY WARBLER

Oporornis formosus

(p. 244)

Habitat: Rich, moist deciduous and mixed woodlands, often with heavy ground cover.
Often sings from the forest understory.
Voice: Song a loud, whistled *chur-ry, chur-ry, chur-ry* . . .
Notes:

CAROLINA WREN

Thryothorus ludovicianus

(p. 214)

Habitat: Thickets and other heavy undergrowth. This bird's song may be heard throughout the year.
Voice: Song extremely variable; a loud and repetitious two- or three-syllable phrase, such as *wheedle, wheedle, wheedle* . . . and *tea-kettle, tea-kettle, tea-kettle* . . . Note the similarity between the songs of the Carolina Wren and the Kentucky Warbler. *Call notes:* A variety of harsh scolding sounds and reedy trills.
Notes:

HOODED WARBLER

Wilsonia citrina

(p. 242)

Habitat: Moist woodlands with heavy undergrowth.
Voice: A ringing, three-phrase song: *a-weet, a-weet, a-weet-teo*. Listen for the emphasis and jump in pitch in the *a-weet-teo* phrase.
Notes:

COMMON YELLOWTHROAT

Geothlypis trichas

(p. 246)

Habitat: A wide range of habitats, usually with brushy cover and often in association with water.
Voice: Song is variable—often a loud *witchety, witchety, witchety*. The notes are connected, which gives a rolling quality to the song. *Call note:* A flat, raspy tchep.
Notes:

YELLOW WARBLER

Dendroica petechia

(p. 238)

Habitat: Wetland thickets as well as upland hedgerows and copses.
Voice: Song a bright, perky *sweet, sweet, sweet, little more sweet*.
Notes:

NORTHERN PARULA

Parula americana

(p. 230)

Habitat: Nests in a wide range of woodland habitats, commonly where Spanish moss or *Usnea* lichen is available for nest building.
Voice: Song a buzzy trill that progressively climbs in pitch and "drops over the top" at the end. Song begins, at times, with an introductory series of notes on one pitch.
Notes:

BLACK-THROATED GREEN WARBLER

Dendroica virens

(p. 230)

Habitat: Open woodlands, including coniferous and mixed forests. Often sings from the treetop canopy.
Voice: Typical songs are a high-pitched *zee, zee, zee, zoo, zee* and a slower, buzzy *trees, trees, murmuring trees*.
Notes:

AMERICAN REDSTART

Setophaga ruticilla

(p. 236)

Habitat: Commonly found in second-growth deciduous woodlands.
Voice: Variable; typical song sounds like *tzee, tzee, tzee, tzeeo*, comprising three high notes similar in pitch and a lower (occasionally higher) final note. At times the final note is barely discernible or absent. Also a repetitious, two-syllable phrase similar to the song of the Black-and-white Warbler. The Redstart sometimes alternates various songs.
Notes:

Thrushes

The thrush family includes several of North America's premier vocalists. The three woodland species included here all have beautiful, flutelike songs.

WOOD THRUSH

Hylocichla mustelina

(p. 222)

Habitat: Damp, deciduous woodlands; commonly nests in appropriate habitat around human residences. Sings from treetops to perches on or near the forest floor, commonly from relatively low positions.

Voice: Song a series of low introductory notes, followed by a flutelike *ee-o-lay* and ending in a fast-fluttered trill. *Call note:* A clear, loud *pip, pip, pip . . .* , often given at dusk.

Notes:

VEERY

Catharus fuscescens

(p. 222)

Habitat: A wide variety of woodland areas, including low, wet swamps, thickets, and dry hillsides. Often sings from a perch near the ground in heavy cover.
Voice: A downward-spiraling series of phrases; the song has a ventriloquial quality that makes its singer difficult to locate. *Call note:* A repeated, down-slurred *veer* or *wheeu*.
Notes:

HERMIT THRUSH

Catharus guttatus

(p. 222)

Habitat: A variety of woodlands, most often in areas with conifers. Often sings from a perch near the treetops.
Voice: Song begins with a relatively long, low note, followed by a series of tremolo-like phrases; there is considerable variation in pitch from one phrase to the next. *Call notes:* Various, including a soft, low *chuck*; also a plaintive *quee*.
Notes:

Unusual Vocalizations

These three species are grouped together because of the unusual aspects of their songs.

RUFFED GROUSE

Bonasa umbellus

(p. 144)

Habitat: Normally deciduous woodlands during the breeding season, particularly forested areas with dense understory, ranging from wooded hillsides to swampy bottomlands. Typically drums on a log or other prominent perch on or near the ground.

Voice: Song substitute a deep drumming sound; the tempo accelerates through the performance. *Call notes:* Not normally heard; various chucks as well as a *quit-quit* alarm.

Notes:

AMERICAN WOODCOCK

Scolopax minor

(p. 124)

Habitat: Wet areas, including openings in the forest, alder thickets, and river meadows. Sings on and above its breeding territory, most often at dusk and/or dawn.

Voice: A series of nasal *peent* notes on the ground; also a high-pitched wing whir that accompanies the bird's spiraling ascent; descent characterized by various chips and chirps. (See also "Simple Vocalizations," p. 35.)

Notes:

AMERICAN BITTERN

Botaurus lentiginosus

(p. 104)

Habitat: Sedge, rush, and/or cattail marshes in freshwater, brackish, or saltwater wetlands. Often sings from the dense cover of marshland vegetation.

Voice: A deep, repetitious *woonk-ka-chunk*.

Notes:

Miscellaneous Vocalizations

This group includes four fairly common species that do not fit into any of the other groups.

CHIMNEY SWIFT

Chaetura pelagica

(p. 204)

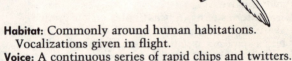

Habitat: Commonly around human habitations. Vocalizations given in flight.
Voice: A continuous series of rapid chips and twitters.
Notes:

WHITE-EYED VIREO

Vireo griseus

(p. 228)

Habitat: Moist thickets and tangles.
Voice: An emphatic *chick-per-a-weeo-chick* or *chick-per-a-weeoo*. Note the *chick* phrase common to most variations of the song.
Notes:

EASTERN BLUEBIRD

Sialia sialis

(p. 220)

Habitat: Agricultural lands, orchards, and open pine woodlots.
Voice: Song is a soft warble with whistles and occasional chattery notes. *Call note:* A musical *chur-wee*, often given in flight.
Notes:

RUFOUS-SIDED TOWHEE

Pipilo erythrophthalmus

(p. 276)

Habitat: Dry areas, including hillsides with second-growth cover, shrubby edges, and thickets. Often heard scratching at leaves on the ground.
Voice: Song comprises two clear, whistled notes followed by a trill, with each of the three phrases being on a different pitch; sounds like *drink your teeeeeee*. *Call note:* A loud *tow-weeee*.
Notes:

CASSETTE 3, SIDE B

Habitat Groupings

See pp. 10–11.

BIBLIOGRAPHY

Audubon Society Master Guide to Birding. 1983. Vols. 1–3. New York: Alfred A. Knopf.

Borror, Donald J. 1967. *Common Bird Songs.* New York: Dover.

———. 1970. *Songs of Eastern Birds.* New York: Dover.

Bull, John, and John Farrand. 1977. *The Audubon Society Field Guide to North American Birds.* New York: Alfred A. Knopf.

Check-list of North American Birds (6th ed.). 1983. American Ornithologists' Union. Lawrence, Kansas: Allen Press.

Cornell Laboratory of Ornithology. 1983. *A Field Guide to Bird Songs of Eastern and Central North America.* Boston: Houghton Mifflin.

Forbush, Edward H., and John B. May. 1939. *Natural History of the Birds of Eastern and Central North America.* Boston: Houghton Mifflin.

Kricher, John C., and Gordon Morrison. 1988. *A Field Guide to Eastern Forests.* Boston: Houghton Mifflin.

Leahy, Christopher. 1982. *The Birdwatcher's Companion: An Encyclopedic Handbook of North American Birdlife.* New York: Hill and Wang.

Peterson, Roger Tory. 1980. *A Field Guide to the Birds of Eastern and Central North America.* Boston: Houghton Mifflin.

Pough, Richard H. 1946, 1949. *Audubon Land Bird Guide.* Garden City, New York: Doubleday.

———. 1951. *Audubon Water Bird Guide.* Garden City, New York: Doubleday.

Robbins, Chandler S., Bertel Bruun, and Herbert S. Zim. 1983. *Birds of North America.* New York: Golden Press.

Saunders, Aretas A. 1935. *A Guide to Bird Songs.* New York: D. Appleton–Century.

Scott, Shirley L., editor. 1983. *Field Guide to the Birds of North America.* National Geographic Society. Washington, D.C.

Stokes, Donald W. 1979. *A Guide to the Behavior of Common Birds.* Boston–Toronto: Little, Brown.

Terres, John K. 1980. *The Audubon Society Encyclopedia of North American Birds.* New York: Alfred A. Knopf.

ALPHABETICAL INDEX

Bittern, American, 57
Blackbird, Red-winged, 47
Bluebird, Eastern, 59
Bobolink, 37
Bobwhite, Northern, 43
Cardinal, Northern, 28
Catbird, Gray, 14
Chickadee(s), Black-capped, 40
    Carolina, 41
Chuck-will's-widow, 40
Cowbird, Brown-headed, 26
Crow, American, 46
Dove, Mourning, 33
Finch(es), House, 43
    Purple, 44
Flicker, Northern, 17
Flycatcher(s), Acadian, 34
    Great Crested, 34
Goldfinch, American, 38
Goose, Canada, 45
Grackle, Common, 48
Grosbeak, Rose-breasted, 21
Grouse, Ruffed, 56
Hawk(s), Broad-winged, 22
    Red-shouldered, 23
    Red-tailed, 23
Heron, Green-backed, 36
Jay, Blue, 46
Junco, Dark-eyed, 25
Killdeer, 42
Kingbird, Eastern, 27
Kingfisher, Belted, 18
Meadowlark, Eastern, 30
Mockingbird, Northern, 13
Night-Heron, Black-crowned, 36
Nuthatch, White-breasted, 35
Oriole(s), Northern, 29
    Orchard, 45
Ovenbird, 49
Owl(s), Barred, 32
    Great Horned, 32
Parula, Northern, 52
Pheasant, Ring-necked, 37
Phoebe, Eastern, 41
Redstart, American, 53
Robin, American, 19
Screech-Owl, Eastern, 33
Sparrow(s), Chipping, 24
    Field, 30
    House, 47
    Song, 48
    Swamp, 24
    White-throated, 31
Starling, European, 27
Swift, Chimney, 58
Tanager(s), Scarlet, 20
    Summer, 20
Thrasher, Brown, 14
Thrush(es), Hermit, 55
    Wood, 54
Titmouse, Tufted, 29
Towhee, Rufous-sided, 59
Veery, 55
Vireo(s), Red-eyed, 21
    Warbling, 44
    White-eyed, 58
    Yellow-throated, 22
Warbler(s), Black-and-white, 49
    Black-throated Green, 53
    Hooded, 51
    Kentucky, 50
    Pine, 25
    Yellow, 52
Waxwing, Cedar, 26
Whip-poor-will, 39
Woodcock, American, 35, 57
Woodpecker(s), Downy, 15
    Hairy, 15
    Pileated, 17
    Red-bellied, 16
    Red-headed, 16
Wood-Pewee, Eastern, 42
Wren(s), Carolina, 50
    House, 38
Yellowthroat, Common, 51

PHONETIC INDEX

Ank, ank, ank — White-breasted Nuthatch, 35
A-weet, a-weet, a-weet-teo — Hooded Warbler, 51
Bob white, bob white — Northern Bobwhite, 43
Bubble, bubble, zee — Brown-headed Cowbird, 26
Caw, caw, caw — American Crow, 46
Cheer — Northern Cardinal, 28
Cheerily, cheer-up, cheerily — American Robin, 19
Chick-a-dee-dee-dee — Black-capped Chickadee, 40, and Carolina Chickadee, 41
Chick-burr — Scarlet Tanager, 20
Chick-per-a-weeo-chick or *chick-per-a-weeo* — White-eyed Vireo, 58
Chink — Rose-breasted Grosbeak, 21
Chiva, chiva, chiva — Tufted Titmouse, 29
Chuck-will's-widow — Chuck-will's-widow, 40
Churr, churr, churr — Red-bellied Woodpecker, 16
Chur-ry, chur-ry, chur-ry — Kentucky Warbler, 50 (see also Carolina Wren, 50)
Chur-wee — Eastern Bluebird, 59
Conqueree — Red-winged Blackbird, 47
Dee, dee, dee (separate) — Killdeer, 42
Dee-dee-dee (rapid) — Black-capped Chickadee, 40, and Carolina Chickadee, 41
Drink your teeeeeee — Rufous-sided Towhee, 59
Dtzee, dtzee, dtzeet — Eastern Kingbird, 27
Ee-o-lay — Wood Thrush, 54
Fee-bee (sneezelike) — Eastern Phoebe, 41
Fee-bee (whistled) or *fee-bee-ee* — Black-capped Chickadee, 40
Fee-bee bee-bay — Carolina Chickadee, 41
Fee-b-lee — Eastern Phoebe, 41
Here, here, here — Tufted Titmouse, 29
Here I am, where are you? — Red-eyed Vireo, 21
Jay, jay, jay — Blue Jay, 46
Keeeeeeeeer — Red-tailed Hawk, 23 (see also Blue Jay, 46)
Kee-yer, kee-yer, kee-yer — Red-shouldered Hawk, 23 (see also Blue Jay, 46)
Kik, kik, kik — Pileated Woodpecker, 17
Kill-deer, kill-deer or *ki-dee, ki-dee* — Killdeer, 42
Kleeyer — Northern Flicker, 17
Madam, who cooks for you? — Barred Owl, 32
Maids, maids, maids, put on your tea, kettle, kettle, kettle — Song Sparrow, 48
Meeoow — Gray Catbird, 14
Old Sam Peabody, Peabody, Peabody — White-throated Sparrow, 31
Pee-a-wee or *pee-ee* — Eastern Wood-Pewee, 42

63

Peeeeeeeeee — Broad-winged Hawk, 22 (see also Blue Jay, 46)
Peent, peent, peent — American Woodcock, 35, 57
Peet-seet or *peet-suh* — Acadian Flycatcher, 34
Pee-yer — Eastern Wood-Pewee, 42
Perchickaree — American Goldfinch, 38
Phoe-bee — Eastern Phoebe, 41
Piki-tuki-tuck – Summer Tanager, 20
Plink, plink — Bobolink, 37
Prrreet — Great Crested Flycatcher, 34
Purty, purty, purty — Northern Cardinal, 28
Queedle, queedle, queedle — Blue Jay, 46
Queer, queer — Red-headed Woodpecker, 16
Quwalk, quwalk — Black-crowned Night-Heron, 36
Sam Peabody, Peabody, Peabody — White-throated Sparrow, 31
Skeeow — Green-backed Heron, 36
Spring of the year — Eastern Meadowlark, 30
Sweet, sweet, sweet, a little more sweet — Yellow Warbler, 52
Teacher, teacher, teacher — Ovenbird, 49
Tea-kettle, tea-kettle, tea-kettle — Carolina Wren, 50
Three-a, three-a — Yellow-throated Vireo, 22
Tow-weeee — Rufous-sided Towhee, 59
Trees, trees, murmuring trees — Black-throated Green Warbler, 53
Tseer, tseer — Red-winged Blackbird, 47
Tzee, tzee, tzee, tzeeo — American Redstart, 53
Veer — Veery, 55
Weesa, weesa, weesa — Black-and-white Warbler, 49 (see also American Redstart, 53)
Wheep, wheep, wheep — Great Crested Flycatcher, 34
Wheer — Orchard Oriole, 45
Wheet — Northern Cardinal, 28
Whip-poor-will — Whip-poor-will, 39
Who cooks for you? who cooks for you (all)? — Barred Owl, 32
Who's awake? me too; who's awake? me too — Great Horned Owl, 32
Wick, wick, wick — Northern Flicker, 17
Witchety, witchety, witchety — Common Yellowthroat, 51
Woonk-ka-chunk — American Bittern, 57
Zee, zee, zee, zoo, zee — Black-throated Green Warbler, 53
Zeee, zeee — Cedar Waxwing, 26
Zree — House Finch, 43